BY VINCENT P. COLLINS

This pamphlet is a companion of *Acceptance,* by the same author. It is simple and direct advice about the feelings of inadequacy and discouragement many of us have in the face of the difficulties we meet in our daily lives.

ISBN: 978-0-87029-076-3
COPYRIGHT 1962, REPRINTED 2011
*St. Meinrad Archabbey, St. Meinrad, Indiana*

ABBEY PRESS PUBLICATIONS
ST. MEINRAD, IN 47577

THIS BOOKLET may not be for you. It is not intended for successful, self-reliant, capable, assured people—especially not for "self-made" people. If you happen to be one of the fortunate few who are the "Captains of Their Souls," the "Masters of Their Fate," don't waste your time on it. It is intended for the person who has just never been able to accomplish much, or who used to be able to handle things pretty well, but just can't seem to get any place anymore. If you are finding life increasingly difficult, frustrating, or wearisome, you may find this booklet helpful. If you are really beat, washed up, "tired of livin' and feared of dyin'," you have nothing to lose, so read on.

## The Camel's Back

"What's happened to me?" Perhaps it's the same thing that has happened to thousands of other people, competent, able, mature people. We might call it "the straw that broke the camel's back." Remember the famous "last straw"? Let's recall that sad little tale, and let's say you're the camel, an innocent little camel. When you were a teen-age camel, everybody— Papa, Mama, Teacher, Editor, Preacher, and especially the Commencement Speaker—all dinned the same thing into your receptive little ears: "There's no limit whatsoever to what an honest, resourceful, hardworking camel can do. You can do anything you make up your mind to do. 'The Sky's the Limit.' 'This is the Land of Opportunity.' 'Hitch Your Wagon to a Star,' etc." Nobody ever whispered into your young ear the ugly truth about "The Straw That Broke the Camel's Back." When some battle-scarred old veteran camel finally tried to tell you about it, you refused to believe it. Even when you saw it happening to others, you said, "Well, it can't happen to me!" But it has!

You may think that there was a final straw that did it. Actually, you can't blame "the final straw" any more than you can blame any single one of the countless straws that have been building up the load since childhood. The important thing is that the camel's back is broken. And why shouldn't it be? You have been overloading it for years, and it has finally given out. But never mind that—what are we going to do about it?

## Do It Yourself?

Are you a "Do-it-yourself" enthusiast? Many people look upon life itself as a "Do-it-yourself" project. Like the poor camel in our story, they are convinced that all by themselves they should be able to accomplish anything they put their mind to, providing they work hard enough. They really believe that Commencement oratory. So if they don't succeed, they feel that there must be something wrong with them. That is not so. Living is just too big a proposition for anyone, no matter how capable or self-reliant he may be, to handle by himself. It is not and cannot be a Do-it-yourself project, a one-man operation. Very much to the contrary, living is essentially a partnership.

In all honesty, we must admit that the business of living involves dependence on countless other human beings. Every human being depends on other human beings, even for the basic needs of his daily existence—the butcher, the baker, the candlestick maker, to say nothing of the television repairman. Furthermore, loath as we are to admit this dependence on other human beings, we are even more reluctant to admit our dependence on the One Whom we need most of all—the very Source of our being!

We know that ultimately we owe our existence to our Maker, but we rarely think much about it. God created us, and "That's all there is to it." But that is *not* all there is to it. His creating action did not stop with the moment of our conception. Every single moment since then, He has been keeping us in existence, from one split second to the next. He created us out of nothing, and if He were to withdraw His sustaining action for one moment we would cease to exist. We are absolutely dependent upon him from moment to moment, for every breath, for every heartbeat, for every wink of the eye.

And that's not all. Our dependence upon Him is not limited merely to our continual physical existence. We need His unfailing help in everything, in every undertaking, physical, mental, or spiritual, great or small.

Because God arranged things this way, not only do we need His help, we also have a right to ask for it and to obtain it. After all, He created us without our asking; He is responsible for us. People who bring children into the world take it as a matter of course that they are responsible for their welfare. As a matter of fact, parents derive a great deal of satisfaction in providing for their children the necessities of life—food, clothing, shelter, and the rest. Why then should we deny God, the Parent Supreme, the prerogatives of the human parent? As the Father par excellence, He is happy to provide for the needs of His Children. "Ask and you shall receive."

## Speak up!

We cannot "go it alone." Nobody can. When I say, "I can stand on my own two feet, I can make it on my own," I may really believe it. Actually, however, my brave boast sounds like the cry of a little boy who is afraid of the dark and too proud to admit it. God does not expect us to "go it alone." He knows that we need His help and is eager to help us. At the same time, being the perfect Father, He won't butt into our affairs unless He is asked. Unfortunately, all too often He is not asked.

We offer various reasons for not asking His help. Sometimes we say, "We don't like to bother Him with our insignificant little problems." None of our problems is insignificant to His loving gaze. To Him, no problem is too large to solve or too small to bother with. Even if our problem is so weighty that it is driving us to distraction, we may hesitate to call on the grounds that we "feel unworthy or guilty."

"Who would have the gall," we ask, "to ask a favor of someone whom they have offended?" For our own part, we know that if one of our friends has treated us badly, we feel hurt and angry. Furthermore, we are convinced that we have every right to feel that way. Then, if we condescend to accept his apology and forgive him, we think we are being mighty noble. And if we go so far as to return good for evil, that calls for wings and a halo. It is perfectly natural for *us* to react to injury in this way, and it is perfectly natural to believe that *God* reacts in the same way. But the fact is, He doesn't!

But in this matter, we must stop judging God by ourselves. He loves His children with an infinite love; that is, with a love without limits. That love cannot be affected, altered, diminished, or destroyed by anything we do. This means, in effect, that He does not stop loving us when we offend Him. Further, He keeps on loving us even while we persist in offending Him and refuse to repent.

Our loving Father puts up with our weakness, fickleness, stupidity and downright malice even though, in His infinite justice, He will not and cannot condone it. He is always ready to forgive us, providing only that our repentance is sincere. To be honest about it, we can never plead shame or guilt as an excuse for refusing His help.

## Helpless, Not Hopeless

The man who thought up the slogan, "You don't have to be crazy to work here, but it helps!" deserved to make a fortune . Everyone, be he rag-picker or VIP, thinks it was meant just for him. For our purposes, it might well read thus: "You don't have to be helpless to get by, but it helps!" Admitting one's helplessness certainly does help; indeed, it may make all the difference between a happy life and an unhappy one. Remember the other slogan, "It pays to be ignorant?" It also pays to be helpless—ask any woman motorist with a flat.

At some time or other, you may have been up against a problem that was beyond your power to solve. When you mentioned it to a friend, much to your surprise and relief, he jumped right in and began to work out a solution. Philosophers explain this by saying that goodness tends to spread itself. A good person cannot resist the appeal of helplessness. God is

11

Goodness Personified. Being All-good, He wants to help us. Being All-wise, He knows how to help us. Being All-powerful, He can help us. He loves us, in short, and is eager to help us. But remember: He likes to be asked!

Our admission of helplessness gives us an unanswerable claim on the infinite benevolence and power of God. As St. Paul puts it, "Of myself, I can do nothing.... I can do all things in Him who strengthens me." This statement is no mere pious platitude; it is the rock-bottom basis of a complete way of life, the only way of life that makes sense when the chips are down. In it St. Paul states in the plainest possible terms God's divine plan for you and for me: partnership with Him.

## How?

How do I go about making my helplessness, my inadequacy work for me? It makes no difference whether I feel inadequate in one particular area of life only, or in the whole business of living itself; the procedure is the same. The only pre-requisite is that what I want to do is something that must be done. That is, it must be something that my duty to myself, to God, or to others requires me to do. (This will not work for a world cruise, a Bermuda vacation, or even a Cadillac!)

For example, suppose I am a teacher fresh from State Teachers', facing for the first time a class of rough and tough teen-agers noted for their ability to swallow new teachers alive. I feel, with reason, that the situation is beyond my powers. But it has to be done, and I have to do it. I tell God that I doubt that I can do it, or even that I am convinced I can't. Then I ask Him to help me do it, or, if you will, to do it for me. Finally—and this is essential—I pitch in and do my level best. knock myself out. As the saying has it, "Remember that everything depends on God, but work as if everything depended on you." It will be up to Him to see it through, and He will if that happens to be best for me. If it isn't, He will substitute something that is.

## "The Firm"

We have mentioned a partnership. You have just seen a practical example of how it operates. Now let's see just what it involves. A partnership is a working agreement between two individuals in a common enterprise, in which each contributes his share of capital or labor and shares equally in the proceeds.

The partnership we are proposing is unique. God is the Senior Partner in the firm and I am the Junior Partner. Each of us makes his contribution, but by the nature of things His is far greater than mine. That is to say, about 99% of the results are due to His efforts. The same holds true in regard to sharing the proceeds: He is content with a far smaller share than mine. He is the Boss of the operation, so to speak, and I am the legman. He does most of the planning and lays out the work. Although He never appears on the scene in Person, He has many ways of making His presence felt.

Most of the time He leaves things pretty much up to the Junior Partner, but occasionally He may decide to step in and get something done without Junior's efforts—or perhaps, even despite them. This is, after all, His prerogative; for we must never lose sight of the fact that He is the Father of the Junior Partner.

## The Agreement

Most partnership agreements are drawn up once for all and filed away. Not so this one. It is set up every day, and perhaps renewed several times a day, but never for more than one day at a time. The first thing every morning, I initiate the agreement by saying. "Dear Lord, I don't feel able to get through this day by myself. I

15

know you can enable me to do it. Please do. I place my life in your care, just for today. I am at your disposal; please take care of me." That does it; the partnership is in effect from that moment.

If your days are always too full for you to renew your partnership very often during the day, you can still be assured of God's fidelity to the agreement. Your morning prayer can remind God to preserve the partnership always: "O Lord, You know how busy I must be this day. If I forget You, do not You forget me."

If it is not your whole life situation that is too much for you, but just one element in your daily life, amend your agreement to specify that particular element. For example, if you have an uncontrollable temper, put it this way: "Dear God, I can't seem to control my temper. Please enable me to keep my temper, just for today. I place myself and my life in your hands, etc." Then, when the situation that you ordinarily

16

can't handle comes up, renew your morning agreement: "Dear God, I place this situation or undertaking in your hands."

## The Senior Partner

For His part, the Senior Partner agrees to take care of me. That is, He will see to it that nothing happens to me today that could be harmful, in the long run, to me or mine. I must realize, however, that when I turn my life over to Him it may be managed quite differently from the way I would manage it. For one thing, I can't see beyond my nose; whereas His view spans all time and eternity. For another thing, my standard of values is quite different from His, although, as our partnership progresses, I will find myself seeing things more and more through His eyes, and making His standard of values my own.

The Senior Partner's contribution consists of infinite love, infinite wisdom, and infinite power. And in return, He receives the joy of sharing His infinite benevolence with us and the satisfaction of making His loved ones happy. That, after all, is the supreme joy of perfect love.

## The Junior Partner

For my part, I acknowledge my total or partial helplessness. I ask God to help me. I freely place my life in His care. I ask Him to "run it for me." Then I roll up my sleeves and go to work. I do my best, and let Him do the rest. He is pleased with this arrangement, because when I say, "I need you, My God," and ask Him to help me, I am acknowledging in a practical and utterly sincere way my dependence upon Him as my Creator.

My daily contract with God requires certain stipulations on my part. When I place myself and my life in His hands, I am denying myself the luxury of questioning, criticizing or complaining about anything that may happen to me in the course of the day. No matter what He may send down the line, bill collectors, spiteful neighbors, cranky bosses, careless drivers, spoiled children, hurricanes, or whatever, I must learn to accept them as part of His program for me today. "Father knows best!"

Even implied criticism is out. You know, when most people say, for instance, "But why does it have to happen to me?" they really don't want to know why; that's their sneaky way of complaining. More than that, it's a subtle way of criticizing the Boss. So I must stop asking "Why? ? ? Why this, why that, why the other thing, why do they, why does she, etc., etc...?" One querulous "WHY?" is enough to suspend the partnership for the time being. (And by the way, if you *must* know "Why," the answer is simple: "Why?" "Because that's the way it is! Because that's part of His Big Plan!")

## Fringe Benefits

These stipulations, at first glance, might seem designed to take the joy out of life. As time goes on, however, you will find that they have the opposite effect. This way of living opens up a whole new life, a whole new world, a world of light and peace. When I give up the frustrating, worrisome and losing battle of trying to run my life in my own way, I gain abiding peace and deep serenity. You may not believe this until you have actually tried it. So please withhold your judgment until you have. Look at it this way: there are only two wills in the world, mine and God's. Whatever is under my direct control is my will; whatever is beyond my direct control is His Will. My partnership teaches me to accept that which is beyond my control as God's will for me. As time goes on, I come to realize that in surrendering my will to the divine Will, I am for the first time living without turmoil and without anxiety.

## Who's Boss?

It should not be necessary to point out that obedience to the wishes of the Senior Partner must be a prerequisite to our agreement. Nevertheless, perhaps it should be spelled out: God has a right to expect that, in return for His help, I will do my best not to offend Him. Therefore I must strive to do whatever I believe He wants me to do and to avoid doing whatever I believe He doesn't want me to do.

But how am I to find out what He expects of me? I ask Him in prayer: "Lord, what wouldst Thou have me do?" I consult His explicit Will as He has revealed it in the Ten Commandments and in the New Testament, particularly in the Sermon on the Mount. I already know what my daily duties are, and I discharge them to the best of my ability. Beyond that, when a choice between two courses of action is offered, I can make a fairly accurate guess as to which would be more pleasing to Him.

If I strive always to be *honest with myself,* I may be confident that my choice will be the right one.

## Pie in the sky?

At this point, some cynic will raise his sardonic head and observe, "Be honest, now, and admit that what you really are driving at is that all a person has to do is to want something, whine that he can't get it on his own, pray sadly, and then sit back until it arrives on a silver platter. Isn't that about it?" No, it isn't! Granting that the Senior Partner does 99% of the work, our 1% is still essential. He may do practically all of the effective work, but he expects the Junior Partner to do a real job. "God helps those who help themselves."

Put it this way: Spotty, the new puppy on the block, brags to the other dogs, "Say, you guys, did you know that I can open our big front door just by scratching on it? Pretty clever, hey?" Old Bassett gently replies, "Look, kiddo, I hate to tell you this, but you don't really open the door. What happens is, they hear you scratching and *they* open it. See?" Spotty comes back: "Yeah, but if I don't scratch, it won't open. And that's enough for me. What more do you want?" Yes, what more do you want? This much we'll grant the cynic though, we do have to scratch on the door.

In other words, after I have asked God's help, it's up to me to pitch in and do my best. But (and this is a very important "but,") it has to be my best; not my almost best or second best. It must be absolute and unqualified best. Then, if it be for my good, I shall succeed. Otherwise, I may not. It is not for me to worry about results; that's up to the Senior Partner. Once I am convinced that I have made every possible effort, I have succeeded, regardless of the outcome.

No cynic worth his cyanide would be put off by this answer. Nor is he: "So you equate success with doing your best? Ridiculous! Suppose you do your very best and still fall flat on your face? What then? Claim a moral victory? Moral victories don't bring home the bacon or pay the rent!"

## Success and Failure

Let's take a quick look at the notion of success. The greatest mistake one can make about success is to confuse it with happiness. The dictionary defines success as "the attainment of an objective." That means reaching a goal, accomplishing a desired end. Success may bring happiness, but only insofar as the goal or objective is something that is *capable of making us happy.* The joke is that what we *think* will make us happy and what really *will* make us happy are often two different things. If our goal is right for us, achieving it will make us happy. If it is the wrong one, achieving it will not make us happy; it may bring us frustration, disappointment, and perhaps even misery. Remember King Midas?

Only God can know with certainty what would constitute success for any particular individual, since He alone has the requisite accurate and exhaustive knowledge of the person and the circumstances. Being the only one who can know a person inside out, He alone can know what goals would make that person happy.

Most people believe that success consists in the attainment of wealth, power or pleasure. Even when men who have attained them try to convince us that it just isn't so, we listen politely and say, "Okay, maybe so. But give *me* a crack at that wealth, etc., and let me find out for myself!" Human nature being what it is, our chances of choosing the right objectives are pretty slim. But if we leave the day-by-day direction of our lives up to God, we have a very good chance of achieving happiness. As for success, we are successful if we are content with what we are and with what we have. Pity the poor soul—and his number is legion— who is truly a success and doesn't know it!

At any rate, we have no business trying to decide for ourselves whether we are a "success or a "failure." We won't find out for sure until judgment day. Nor should we worry too much about how other people evaluate us; chances are that their guess is no better than our own. Ponder this cheerful sentiment about the "successful man": "His ambition is to be the richest man in the cemetery!"

## Worry

Success or failure may be the least of your worries. You may even be worried silly precisely because you have nothing to worry about. ("This is too good to last.") Most of us, however, have plenty of real, tangible worries: money or health, death and taxes. Now, the antidote to worry and fear is confidence; confidence not in ourselves, but in our Partner. We must believe that He can and will avert the calamity that we spend our days and nights dreading. If it should nevertheless happen to us, we must believe that He will enable us to weather it and to be better for it.

To give us our due, we worry not so much about ourselves as about those who depend upon us. We think so often, "What would happen to my wife, my family, my business, or whatever, if anything should happen to me?" The implication is that their welfare depends entirely upon us. It does, but only *under God.* It depends immediately upon us, but ultimately upon Him. He uses us to take care of our loved ones, it is true, but that doesn't mean that He needs us. We can be replaced!

If you are a parent, you may say, "But don't my children need me?" Certainly they do, under the present circumstances. At the same time, has it ever occurred to you that actually you need them more than they need you? You may not like this thought, but it's true: God made you a parent less for the sake of your children than for your own sake. You need to be a parent more than they need to be *your* children. (For that matter, there are thousands, if not millions, who could do your job much better than you.) This holds not only for parents, but for doctors, judges, clergymen, bricklayers and presidents. Brutally put, "Who needs you?!!"

"Why, then...?" That answer is this: life is a partnership, remember? And your contribution is only a tiny 1%, an essential 1%, but essential only *to you.* Must we take the weight of the whole world, or even of our own little world on our shoulders? They weren't built for it, as St. Christopher found out. We must stop trying to play God. As a friend of mine in the building trades likes to put it: "Management is paid to do the worrying. I just lay the bricks!"

## "Thank you!"

Now, a final word about gratitude. One of the wisest men I know insists that the best measure of a man's character is his capacity for feeling and expressing gratitude. You may be familiar with the cynical definition of gratitude: "The expectation of further favors." Some people even profess to believe that ingratitude is an inborn human trait. But it would seem that we are actually not so much ungrateful as thoughtless. When things are rough and we are close to desperation, we are pitifully grateful for the least little help. Then, as things get better, we tend to forget our desperation and with it, the people who came to our rescue.

Pity though it is, it does seem true that we are inclined to let time gloss over our consciousness of the debt we owe to the One Who never failed us in our time of trial, the One Who saves our well-being, sanity, or perhaps our very life. It is necessary, then, to point out that the partnership which is initiated every morning with a "Please" must be sealed every night with a "thank You!"

Not that our Senior Partner needs our gratitude; but *we* need to be grateful and we need to express our gratitude. Therefore: "You have given us this day our daily bread; You have forgiven us our trespasses; You have delivered us from evil. Hallowed be Thy Name, now and forever. Amen."

O Lord,

You know how busy

I must be this day:

If I forget You,

Do not You forget me.

Prayer of Sir Jacob Astley
before the battle of Edgehill.

**B**ack in print by popular demand, *Partnership* is filled with simple, direct advice for anyone with feelings of inadequacy and discouragement. From the author of the best-selling title, *Acceptance,* this pamphlet points the way to happiness and fulfillment through dependence on God.

95¢

#11087

**Abbey Press**
**St. Meinrad, IN**
**47577**

ISBN 978-0-87029-076-3

9 780870 290763

00095